# Can I achieve more in life?

## more in life?

Assisting men and women
rediscover their purpose in life

# DUVILÈNE PIETER

## With EUNICE ANITA

The Netherlands

**Can I achieve more in life?**
MY PURPOSE-SERIES
Copyright © 2019 Duvilène Pieter with Eunice Anita
Published by Highly Favored Publishing
www.highlyfavored.nl

Motivational
Paperback ISBN 978-94-92266-16-3
E-Book Epub ISBN 978-94-92266-17-0
BISAC OCC019000, REL012070
NUR 707, 740

# Contents

Contents .......................................................1

Introduction .................................................3

Affirming statements.....................................5

Being a champion .........................................7

The foundation.............................................9

God's perfect will ........................................13

One's purpose in life ...................................15

Guarding the heart ......................................19

Feeling Stuck ..............................................23

Your Purpose is not mine .............................27

Born to rule ................................................31

Demolish the barriers...................................33

Can I achieve more? ....................................37

Notes .........................................................41

About the authors ........................................49

Other publications........................................51

# Introduction

This booklet titled, **Can I Achieve More in Life,** is an invitation to you for a journey centered on achieving more in life by underlining and knowing who you are. Have you (really) asked yourself the question: **Who am I? Who was I created to be?**

Life is a journey containing many phases. We all started as a baby, the daughter or son of, and have evolved into a teenager, student, father, mother, husband, wife, unemployed, employee, and will be or already are a senior. So many phases, and so many things one can and may achieve during these phases and transitions. Nevertheless, in all those phases, the essence of being who you are, and of being a beloved person created in the image of God and with a divine purpose, does not change.

Embrace your uniqueness and purpose in Jesus and achieve far more than you may have imagined.

# Affirming statements

I am a human being with a purpose. Out of all the male reproductive cells that were released, I made it, and I am alive today.

I declare with certainty that:

\# I am not an accident, God wanted me to be alive.

\# I am created in the image and likeness of God.

\# By discovering who God is, I learn more of myself, for I am created in His image and likeness.

\# I am created to govern and to rule.

\# The Word of God is my guideline in life.

\# I consist of a body, soul, and spirit, and it is essential to nourish all of them.

\# God's perfect will for my life was described before man sinned.

\# I am part of the Kingdom of God. A Kingdom of Righteousness, Peace, and Joy in the Holy Spirit.

\# I can do all things through Christ that strengthens me.

# Being a champion

Biology teaches us that once upon a time, many male reproductive cells took a journey, and the cell who hits homerun develops into a baby. Every baby is a champion who made it through this journey.

At our conception, we had our first achievement in life, which was becoming a champion. Before this biological action, it was The Creator who spoke and what He said came into existence. The same way in which He said let there be light, and there was light, in that same manner, He said for you to come on earth, and so it was.

When you look at your life, how many things have you spoken with a loud voice or perhaps silently in your mind, which are the reality you live in today?

As human beings, created in the image of God, we have the ability to speak things into existence. Our words become our thoughts, our thoughts become our action, and our actions become our habits, which is the reality we live in.

To be and to remain a champion, one must speak as a champion. Speak words that nurture your spirit, body, and soul.

## *Prayer*

Awesome God, Creator of heaven and earth, thank you for creating me in Your image and likeness. I may not comprehend it with my mind, but I pray that may You enlighten the eyes of my heart so I can understand what it means that I am created in Your image and likeness. I invite you to come in my life and help me to walk in Your truth, so I may achieve all that You have prepared for me before the foundation of the world. Together with Jesus, I am more than a conqueror. I am and will be a champion for Your name to be glorified. I pray in Jesus' Name, Amen.

## *Scripture*

Genesis 1:3,26; Ephesians 1:8; Proverbs 18:21

# The foundation

A building will last for years and decades despite extreme weather conditions and/or climate changes. What is essential to the building in helping it remain standing during storms? That is its foundation. The foundation should be grounded in rocks; otherwise, it will slip away, taking the whole building with it. The more robust the rock, the better. There is no better rock than Jesus Christ Himself, The Word that became flesh. To start the journey of achieving more in life, in the right way, make sure your feet are grounded in Jesus Christ.

Achieving more in life means growing in one area or in several ones. It is like constructing a building. Once the foundation is done, the walls are set, and the top of the ground level is reached. When starting with the first level floor, all the activities deployed when constructing the ground level must be repeated. The difference is that there is now another perspective. Once the first floor is done, it is the turn of the second floor. Again, everything starts from scratch.

So as the process of constructing a building goes, so is our journey in achieving more in life. With every achievement, the opportunity comes to start the trip all over again, but with the starting point at another level and from a different perspective.

Embrace the journey of self-discovery and self-motivation you embarked on, for achieving more in life means also knowing yourself and staying open to being molded for the right reasons and by the right persons. To make all of this possible, your foundation must be solid and well-constructed.

## *Prayer*

Father, I recognize that I might have been focused on achieving more in life from a wrong perspective and with the faulty foundation as a starting point. I ask you for forgiveness. Jesus Christ, I come to You with a humbled heart. I invite You to come and be the foundation of my being and my life. I want to be rooted in You, the everlasting solid rock.

I understand and admit that I need the Holy Spirit at my side as my counselor and guider on the journey of achieving more in life. Holy Spirit, come and show me the way the Lord has prepared for me so I can achieve more and always honor Him in all that I do. I pray in Jesus' Name. Amen.


*Scripture*

Matthew 7:24-27; Luke 6:48; 1 Corinthians 3:10-11; 2 Timothy 2:19

# God's perfect will

In the beginning, the earth was unformed and void. And God started His creation; step by step. On the first day, God said: _**'Let there be light,'**_ _and there was light."_ (Genesis 1:3) On the sixth day, God created Adam and Eve, and God saw that all He created was good. God blessed the men and told them to be fruitful and to have dominion over the earth. On the seventh day, God rested.

God created men and saw that it was good. Men had no clothes on, no house, no car, no degree, no mother, no sister/brother or children. Two naked people were living in unity and harmony with God, themselves, each other, vegetation, and the animals. They lived in a climate where neither sunblock or umbrella nor winter jacket was needed.

The focus should not be on how to become a millionaire as the ultimate achievement in life. Living like a millionaire might be awesome, but more important is to live in the atmosphere of what God entitled as good and as one's purpose.

Focus on unity and harmony with God, yourself, your loved ones, creation, and on doing what is right. Either being a millionaire or having no dime is not the thing to aim for. Instead, aim for achieving all that is God's will for your life. That is the goal to pursue. A significant part of God's perfect will for His creation is the unity and harmony with God himself we read about that had existed before man sinned.

## *Prayer*

Lord, I thank You for Your love. Forgive me, forgive us, all of humanity, for we admit that we have sinned against you and occasionally we still do when we refuse to act according to what You tell us to do. Father, only You can restore obedience to You and Your Word in us.

Lord, I pray that Your will be done in every area of my life. Great King, I love You, and I need You. Be my Lord. I invite you to come and open my eyes to see Your will for my life and give me the strength to achieve all You created me and equipped me for in life. Lord, I pray in Jesus name.

## *Scriptures*

Genesis 1; Jeremiah 29:11; Matthew 6:10

# One's purpose in life

Lord, what is the **purpose** You created me for? Have you asked this question at some point in your life?

Based on what we believed to be our purpose, we set goals for us to achieve. The goals one set when one is a teenager are different from those at the time when one is in the situation of being a student, about to get married, single mom or dad or a widow(er).

I believe that our purpose in life lies in creation. When God created man in His image and likeness, He blessed man and told Him to be fruitful and have dominion over the earth. God is love, and when we live out of love, we live out of our divine nature. When we live out of rage or depression, we are not living in accordance with our true nature.

As life evolves, God guides our steps into our divine purpose. Sometimes, it might be through a desire we have had from our childhood, a dream we had one night, a family or friend that invites us to try something new.

It might also be through a (new) talent we develop, a profession that has been in the family for generations or doors that were (suddenly) shut in front of us. There is no limit on how God can and may lead us into our purpose, His divine destiny for our lives.

Important is for God's will to be the center of the goals we set so we may walk into our divine purpose. I love the prayer Jesus taught his disciples: **"Father Your Kingdom come. Your will be done on earth as it is in heaven…"**. When we are aligned with God's will, we are in line with God's Kingdom, and we have His grace and His ministering angels partnering with us.

*Prayer*

Lord, You are my Father. You have a purpose for me, and You reveal it to me in phases for You know I will not be able to comprehend it all at once. Your Name is to be exalted, and I will do that each and every day. Thank you that I can pray to you as Jesus taught His disciples:

*"Our Father which art in heaven, Hallowed be thy name. Thy kingdom come, Thy will be done in earth, as it is in heaven. Give us this day our daily bread. And forgive us our debts, as we*

*forgive our debtors. And lead us not into temptation, but deliver us from evil: For thine is the kingdom, and the power, and the glory, for ever. Amen*." (Matthew 6: 9-13, KJV)


*Scriptures*

Matthew 6: 9-13; 1 John 4:7-9; Proverbs 18:14

# Guarding the heart

I love this Bible verse "*Above all else, guard your heart, for everything you do flows from it.*" (Proverbs 4:23)

For many years I connected this verse with who I trust my heart to. But, I discovered this verse to be more profound: "*And the peace of God, which passeth all understanding, shall keep your hearts and minds through Christ Jesus.*" (Philippians 4:7)

It is the peace of God that guards our heart. Which means we have to be guardians. As guardians, we identify what steals our peace, and we work to regain it and so our life.

Is there a desire that you are not achieving? Are you working on a purpose that is not your destiny?

King David had the desire to build a house for the Lord, but God told Him that he would not make Him a house. One of his sons would build the temple. King David, before he died, prepared everything and left his son with the instructions.

David had a desire that was not his assignment to fulfill. This unfulfilled desire didn't make him bitter or depressed. His heart stayed in peace, and he did what he could do. When his desire to bring the ark of God into Jerusalem (also known as the city of David) was fulfilled, David celebrated it with all his strength.

On the other hand, we do not see this kind of humility before the Lord in King Saul. When God rejected Saul as King, Saul became full of rage and determined to kill David. He even tried to kill his own son!

When you notice that your divine purpose does not line up with your own desires and plans, guard your heart, and do not become bitter. Accept that the Lord knows what is best for you and rejoice in that which He has equipped you to do.

*Prayer*

Lord, what are the goals that I've set and desires I might have that are not in line with Your will for my life? Lord, what are the reasons that it seems that all doors are closed? I invite you to come and to open the eyes of my understanding for me to see what is not coming from You.

Dear Lord, Creator of heaven and earth, purify my heart of all that steals my peace. Teach me to guard my heart, to identify what takes my peace away and give me the strength and conviction to remove it if possible or deal with it. I pray for your peace that surpasses all understanding.

Give me the serenity, and the wisdom to accept Your will for my life and the strength to fight the good fight of faith to achieve Your will for my life. Lord, I want to walk in your perfect peace. Father, in Jesus' Name, I pray. Amen.

*Scriptures*

Proverbs 4:23; Philippians 4:7;
1 Samuel 20:30-33; 2 Samuel 7:13-16, 6:12-15

# Feeling Stuck

I had a season in my life when I felt stuck. No matter how hard I tried or how hard I worked, I wasn't achieving my goal(s). I was not moving forward. I was just stuck! I remember how I went to a friend's house, and we had a pity party. Isn't it awesome when you can have someone who understands you and together you can complain about everything that's not working the way you want it?

When I went back home, I opened up my Bible spontaneously at Job chapter 38. Little had I known that God would minister to me that it is better to trust Him than to use my energy for complaining.

There might be a season in which you feel that you are stuck, while you are doing all that you can do. Know that it is in such seasons that you are being prepared for the next phase in life. These are the season in which something new is being conceived. 'Friends' depart, making room for new ones, or teaching us the value of friendship. We get molded so we can mature in several areas of our lives. We might even get more understanding for someone else going through difficulties, for we know now how it is to transcend a rough path.

It is easy to believe the lie that in life, we do not have to fight for anything, or that as long as we walk in God's will, we won't have setbacks. Jesus, Who is The Truth, said: "*These things I have spoken unto you, that in me ye might have peace. In the world ye shall have tribulation: but be of good cheer; I have overcome the world.*" (John 16:33, KJV)

Christ and His followers, e.g., Stephanus and Paul, were killed for the sake of the Gospel. As Stephanus was being stoned to death, he saw the heavens getting open, he saw God in His Glory, and he saw Jesus sitting at the right hand of God. Paul knew that he would be killed, yet he hadn't stopped sharing the Gospel. Their story tells us that being in line with God's will means *not being in agreement with* the prince of this world. This teaches us that there is a price to pay. In all of this, we can be of good cheer for Greater is Jesus Who is in us than satan that is in the world.

*Prayer*

Lord thank you for being with me in all seasons of life; in those seasons that all is laughter and I feel that not even the sky is the limit and also when I think that I am stuck and all my efforts are just a waste of time. Lord forgive me for those moments I felt so overwhelmed wondering where you were and believing that you have left me. Forgive me, Lord, for those seasons when I felt that my situation is bigger than You and that I thought that I can face life on my own, without You.

Dear Lord, merciful Father, You say for us to be thankful for all things. You are the Director, and I invite You to come and help me in my moments of unbelieve. I thank You, Father, that all things work together for good for those who love you. Lord, I love You. I want to love You even more. Thank you, Father, that You give me the strength and Your insight in those seasons that I feel stuck. Help me to put my trust in You each and every day in Jesus Name.

*Scriptures*

John 16:33, 14:6; Acts 7:54-59, 21:11-13; John 14:30; Job 38 & 39; Romans 8:28

# Your Purpose is not mine

What if Elijah had said: *I do not want to walk in Camel's hair for I wish to minister as Samuel did!* And what if Paul had said: *I will go to Mount Sinai for God to speak to me as He had spoken to Moses!* Would history be the same? Or, what if Samson had loved Israelite women. Would he have had a reason to be in the enemy's camp to deliver the Israelites from their enemies?

I do not know if history would repeat itself if we position ourselves as someone else had done in the past. What we see in the Bible is that all things work together for good for God's people. The DNA of each human being is different, and God's purpose for everybody is unique. We can find the overall purpose of God for all men outlined and written about before men sinned. We all have our own and unique task to perform in this world.

Walk your journey of achievement in life with peace in your heart and with the assurance that the steps of a righteous man are ordered by God.

I had my list and my time schedule to achieve it all, and I felt stuck when it hadn't come to pass in my time. I made mistakes that made me feel even worse, and that gave me the false assurance that these mistakes were the reason for me being stuck.

But what is this feeling? What is it to feel stuck?

- Is it the absence of achieving something in the scheduled time?
- Is it an area in my life that needs to be mature so I can achieve the goal?
- Am I lazy?
- Am I afraid to do what I know I am supposed to do?
- Is it that my goal is not in line with God's will for my life and He has something better for me?
- Or, is it that I have to fight my good fight of faith?

So many questions. Search in God's presence for the answer to these questions if or when you feel stuck, for nothing in this journey of life is a coincidence.

*Prayer*

Dear Father, thank You for loving me and that Your plans for my life are for good. Forgive me for comparing my life with that of others and feeling so small or unworthy. Forgive me for not taking the time to find out what Your will for my life is.

Jesus, I invite you to come in my life and help me to put my eyes on You and to do things Your way. Help me to function as You have designed me and not to focus on the tasks assigned to others. Lord, You have given to each of us a portion so we may fulfill the tasks assigned to us.

Holy Spirit, help me to walk in my divine purpose and complete the tasks assigned to me in Jesus Name.


*Scriptures*

2 Kings 1:8; Exodus 19:1-3; Judges 14:3; 1 Timothy 6:12; 2 Timothy 1:7

# Born to rule

The Creator said: *"Let us make man in our image, after our likeness: and let them have dominion over the fish of the sea, and over the fowl of the air, and over the cattle, and over all the earth, and over every creeping thing that creepeth upon the earth."* (Genesis 1:26, KJV)

We were created to rule, to be a leader with an assignment, and to live and achieve all by making use of our divine nature for we were created in the image and likeness of God Himself. We are not God, God forbid us to think like that, but as He is the Creator, we have the ability to create. Look around you, and you will see what men created. After many meetings, talking, planning, thinking, and deliberation, it was made. For good or for our own destruction, that is how we, as human beings, have given expressions to our assignment to rule.

Can you achieve more in life? Yes, you can! There is much more to accomplish in life, for God had not set boundaries to what you can achieve.

So, you don't have to put limitations neither permit others to put them for you. Walk in the will of God and achieve all that you were created to accomplish in every area of life; spiritual, emotional, financial, and physical.

## *Prayer*

Lord, thank You for creating me in Your image and likeness. Thank You for the assignment You gave me as a ruler on the earth, for I am born to rule.

Father, I pray that as I walk in life, Your Spirit may walk with me, guiding me and teaching me as Jesus did with His disciples. Holy Spirit, You are welcome in my life. Teach me how to be a ruler on earth that pleases the Father, in Jesus Name.

## *Scriptures*

Genesis 1:26; Jeremiah 29:11; John 14:16-17, 16:7,8

# Demolish the barriers

We all have our paradigm, our belief system that is the foundation we build on. On the other hand, we can also have beliefs that limit us and obstruct us to achieve all that we are created for. It is our duty to recognize and demolish these strongholds, the limitations to our achievements.

Jesus instructed His disciples to stay in Jerusalem and wait for the Spirit of truth, for when they would receive the Spirit of truth, they would also receive power. We read that after the baptism of the Holy Spirit, Peter, who had denied Christ, stood up, spoke boldly, and 3,000 men were added to the followers of Christ.

Entering the temple, Peter said to a beggar, "*I have no silver and gold, but what I do have I give to you. In the name of Jesus Christ of Nazareth, rise up and walk*" (Acts 3:6, ESV)

Holy Spirit was at the beginning of creation. Followers of Christ had to wait on the Holy Spirit to receive Power before they could advance. Hebrews and Gentiles, both, were filled with the Holy Spirit and obtained the power to accomplish God's will.

All you need so you can achieve your purpose in life, shall God provide for you. Demolish the barriers, and rule in the areas you are meant to rule in. Whether you are homeless, single, a mother, a father, a teenager, a student, an entrepreneur, a preacher, a teacher, a billionaire, a member of the government or a (political) prisoner, it does not matter. We are all individually unique and designed to rule in all area of our lives in unique ways.

### *Prayer*

Lord, I come to you as I am, and I invite you to meet with me and reveal to me the parts of my belief systems that are limiting me. Show me the idols I am holding to, knowingly or unknowingly, that are holding me back or deviating me from my walk with Jesus. I pray for revelation on wrongs I have spoken over my life and commitments I made that are withholding me from achieving what I am created to accomplish. I renounce to every harm I have spoken over my life, against my future and progression in life.

In Jesus' Name, I pull down every paradigm or belief system that I may have, which exalts itself above the knowledge of God.

I bring every thought into the captivity to the obedience of Christ.

Lord, please release Your angels assigned to my life, so they can help me to do Your perfect will in every area of my life.

Lord Jesus, be my Lord and Savior. I invite You to rule in every area of my life. Holy Spirit You are welcome in my life. Reveal to me all truth, convince me of sin, righteousness, and justice. Guide me so I can walk in God's will. I want to walk every day in the Spirit and not in the flesh. Amen.

*Scriptures*

John 16:13; Acts 1:4-5 and 8, 2:41, 3:1-8; 2 Corinthians 10:3-5; Philippians 4:8

# Can I achieve more?

Can I achieve more in life, is a question that may ponder once in a while in one's mind. Surely achieving more is possible. Children of God can do all things through Christ that strengthens them. Don't limit yourself in all you can accomplish, for you are created to be victorious in all areas of life.

Victory can be achieved in all area of life being, emotional, financial, physical, and spiritual.

**Emotional achievement**: Walking in God's peace that surpasses all understanding is vital for one's soul. Be that guardian who is alert and violently in demolishing all thoughts, obstacles and (daily) activities that rob you from His peace. Run to the Father and tell Him all that bothers you, all that steals your peace and inner joy. Let Him restore your peace because that is something which only He can do. His Kingdom is a Kingdom of righteousness, peace, and happiness.

Yes, there is more to achieve on the emotional level. Feeling loved, treasured, and save are boosters for one's confidence. Jesus offers them all to you. It is when you have them, that you can share them with others. Go for it, for you are created in the image of God.

**Financial achievement:** if you want to become a millionaire, and that is your divine purpose, go for it and be that millionaire; a Kingdom financial on earth. Job, a true believer, was in his lifetime the richest men in the east. If it is not your divine purpose to become a millionaire in the eyes of men, don't feel bad. Celebrate life for the Apostle Paul suffered hunger, and yet he experienced what it means to have it all. He said that in all of this, he had learned to rejoice and be happy.

Whatever phase your financial situation may be in on this journey of life, you can experience God's peace at all moments. God provides for His children through the riches glory in Jesus Christ.

**Physical achievement:** You have been created in the image and likeness of the Creator. Your body is made to function well and to the fullness of its capabilities. Each phase of life has an average corresponding physical ability related to it. Take good care of your body for God gave you only one, and you will not get another body in this lifetime. Speak life over your body. Do not get stuck on remembering what you were capable of in the past but rejoice for all that you are capable of in each life cycle. Being young is great. Getting matured and elderly is also amazing. Whatever phase you are in on this journey of life, it is essential for God to be central in your life. You can experience God's peace in every phase.

**Spiritual achievement:** God created men, and He communed with men. He gave Adam instructions in accordance with His perfect will for humanity. In the cool of the day, God walked in the garden of Eden. When men sinned, men hide from God, for men was afraid of God.

Jesus came into this world to restore our relationship with God. He is the way to the Father. The Holy Spirit is your helper in prayer and supplication and guides you in your daily walk. Invite the Father, Jesus, and the Holy Spirit into your life. Confess your sin(s), forgive and receive forgiveness and walk in that intimacy with the Creator. A restoration of your relationship with the Father catapults you into your divine purpose with achievements in line with God's Word in all areas of life as a result.

## *Prayer*

Lord, thank You for Your love. Thank You for all I have achieved and all that You will guide me in so I can succeed. I invite You to come and guide me in Your perfect peace.

Give me discernment so I can recognize Your will for my life, and demolish all limits I set or that my culture and belief system has set for me.

Thank you, Father, for providing for me the strength, wisdom, divine connections, and all that is needed for me to complete Your will in my life. In Jesus' Name I pray, Amen.

## *Scriptures*

Philippians 4:8,13; Job 1:3

# Notes

I want to encourage you to write down ideas, prayers, thoughts, plans, that which comes up in your mind when going through this booklet. Use it to inspire yourself as you walk in God's will through all phases of life.

# About the authors

Duvilène Pieter

Duvilène is a professional with a Master's degree in Business Organization and a Bachelor's degree in Electrical Engineering. She is a professional who believes in God and says: *"Lord, here am I, may your will be done in my life."*
In her career she experienced setbacks as a woman in a "man's field", but they have not robbed her of her determination to achieve more in life. This booklet is birthed in her life's journey as *clay in the Potters hand.*

The author wants to transmit that achievement on itself is not or should not be the goal, instead define to go through the journey with a peaceful heart as a goal. We all have different purposes and assignments. What we do or do not achieve in life will not determine who we are for we are all created in the image and likeness of God to rule here on earth.

Different books published by Highly Favored Publishing were reviewed by the author. Now by God's grace, she had the opportunity to write her first booklet. A new area for her to master and to rule for the Glory of God.

Eunice Anita

Eunice, who co-authored this booklet, is also a professional. She has a Masters' degree in Accounting and is well aware that her life had not started at the point of having a masters' degree. To achieve this, she had to work hard and develop skills in several areas of life. While growing up, she learned to value her journey of achieving more in life, naturally and spiritually.

# Other publications

<u>Other booklets in the MY PURPOSE - Series</u>

### *Who am I?*
*Assisting professionals regaining inner joy and peace*
Paperback ISBN 978-94-92266-14-6
E-Book Epub ISBN 978-94-92266-15-9

### *What kind of leader am I?*
*Assisting leaders in rediscover how to lead God's way*
Paperback ISBN 978-94-92266-18-7
E-Book Epub ISBN 978-94-92266-19-4

<u>Other publications of Eunice Anita</u>

### *Stories to tell to show His Greatness*
*God working thru the highly educated*
Paperback ISBN 978-15-04937-17-7
E-Book Epub ISBN 978-15-04937-18-4

Made in the USA
Columbia, SC
26 October 2024

44700833R00033